100 Ways to Make a Difference Right Where You Are
with What You Have

Vau've Anais Davis

This book is dedicated to my grandfather and mom; they are the reason I am the person I am today.

A generous person will prosper; whoever refreshes others will be refreshed.

—Proverbs 11:25

FOREWORD
BY SHAWN NALLS

I'm proud to have met V. An unconventional acquaintance—a digital run-in on some mutual friend's status updates. Her vibe was dope, so I sent her a friend request. From then, I was immediately impressed by her range. She could drop dimes on Lebron's game four performances or switch gears and break down various social elements that reflect a need for change in our community. Our random conversations became a highlight for me. In many ways, it felt as if there was some deeper purpose behind the reason we met.

It wasn't long before I recognized the passion in V. She was eager to make a change. Through our regular exchanges, she learned about my mother's work in DC—founding a community health and human-service agency that provides prevention, care, and support services for low-income women, girls, and families living with or at risk for HIV/AIDS. Without hesitation, she offered to fundraise and organized a toy donation for the agency's annual Christmas party. Humble. Thoughtful.Genuine. These are the words that come to mind when I think of her.

Apparently, the two most important days of your life are the day you are born and the day you find out why. On our personal paths to fulfillment, it's easy to wander into the rat race and become focused on individual goals. Capitalism is a fickle friend. We are constantly in pursuit of her validation; we give up on lifelong dreams just to take a more practical approach in hopes of better getting her attention—even if it's just a wink from the other end of the bar. Too often, our communities suffer because, realistically, we're just not her type. After countless conversations with V, we both agreed that achieving social and economic independence in our communities would require a shift in thinking.

Understandably, family, jobs, bills, and a host of other priorities cause us to retreat further into our own bubbles. The collective struggle is real. One day we will realize that our communities are only as strong as their weakest link. In today's political climate, being our brother's keeper might be more important than ever. Losing sight of this could have unimaginable consequences.

I welcome each of you to take a journey down a path of selflessness. With confidence, I can assure you this book will not only inspire your philanthropist spirit, but also provide unique and creative ways to make a difference. The journey, like all things, will be what you make of it.

ACKNOWLEDGMENTS

Thank you to everyone who has made a contribution to this book with a piece of knowledge, inspiration, or support.

Introduction

I have always tried to find ways to give back to those less fortunate, in any way possible. After watching television shows like *Secret Millionaire* and *Extreme Makeover: Home Edition*, I realized that there are countless small ways we can give back in our own right.

Having worked in the nonprofit sector for over ten years, I have grown to identify "the need," and I'm constantly racking my brain on ways to do something about it. Whether it was with a small grassroots social-service organization, a midsized organization, or a large (celebrity-endorsed) organization with plentiful private funding, I recognized there was always an unmet need.

The small to midsized organizations that had the "numbers" (this refers to the project numbers provided to grant funders to support a document's need for grant funding) needed the funds to accommodate the need. Even with the leanest administrative and support staff and a modest budget, there is a bottom line all organizations need to meet in order to provide a safe and adequate service to its clients. Unfortunately, many grant funds restrict grantees to specific projects, leaving everyday operational needs unmet. Unmet needs can include everything from administrative support to replacing toilet seats. The need for funds is ongoing.

Working with non-for-profit organizations is just one piece to the bigger puzzle I call my ministry. In addition to working with nonprofits, I volunteer quite often, using my consulting firm, Official Anais Consulting, as a conduit for change. I founded Official Anais Consulting, formerly Official Anais PR, in 2010. Since its inception, I have used it as a platform to help develop and promote brands as well as give back. We launched a "Charity Corner"; this blog "corner" was used to feature 501(c)(3) nonprofit organizations and charities. The space was established with the hope of featuring organizations for free in an online forum. Bimonthly, we featured new organizations to help solicit donations for causes that serve communities throughout Illinois and the Greater Chicagoland areas. This was a great opportunity for nonprofits to take advantage of free publicity as well as expand the possibility of donations.

Providing this platform for charities throughout Illinois to receive free publicity was one of the many ways I planned to give back with what I had. Most small nonprofit organizations simply can't afford to hire marketing/PR teams to reach the people necessary to help fund their causes. People learning more about causes that support our communities and building new positive relationships provided hope and inspiration.

In addition to our Charity Corner, we host an annual toy drive that helps provide support to single mothers. It's grown over the years, and we have expanded to helping organizations and parents out of state. This is one of the many projects I've worked on that I take the most pride in. Having been raised by a single mother, I understand the hardships. As a result, I've grown to have a deep empathy for single parents who are trying to make a better life for themselves and their children. Many of the tips you will read in this book will be geared toward single mothers for that reason.

These projects are just a glimpse into the world of a giver. I've come to learn that God provided me with a heart and unique empathy for others. Day in and day out, I constantly try to find ways to give back or make life easier for another person. As I've done so, some people have joined me on my journey. It makes me feel good when people share how the work they see me do inspires them to want to do more. It truly makes my heart smile when people look to me as the "give back" resource. I'm often asked, "What can I do to give back? I want to help, but I don't know where to start." This made me start to see a bigger picture as it relates to giving. There were a lot of people who had interest in giving back but simply didn't know how or where to start. Also, there were so many small ways they could do so that would empower them to make a difference. Growing up, I really only saw two spectrums of giving. First was the small-scale, "clean your closet and give away what you no longer need to someone in need" giving. Then there was the "write a big check" type of giving. Having grown up with these limited visions of giving, I found myself working toward a certain academic level and socioeconomic status in an effort to be the next Oprah. Oprah has always been a major source of philanthropic inspiration for me; however, she is rich. Would I have to work the rest of my life to try and become rich in order to give back how I desired to? Would I have to start a school in Africa in order to make a "big difference"? One day I had an epiphany, and the answer to these questions was no. The answer is no for me and you! We all have the power to make a difference in the lives of those who need it most. No matter if you make minimum wage or if you make six figures, my intention with *100 Ways to Make a Difference Right Where You Are with What You Have* is to empower you to give right where you are with what you have—and if you already give above and beyond, to get creative and think outside the box.

I've purposely left space between each tip for you to take notes or journal as you read. Start your dynamic giving journey today.

I believe we each have different passions, gifts, and resources, and because I also believe that we are one, I feel it's extremely selfish, maybe even unnatural, not to use your resources to advance our oneness.

—Renita Manley-Garrett, MPA, executive director of The Arts of Humanity

1. Create or buy small gifts with positive notes of affirmation for children at adoption agencies.

2. Purchase a week's worth of groceries for a senior citizen.

3. Purchase gas and bus cards to give to single mothers.

4. Instead of using a discount on high-priced shoes, buy bulk kids' shoes and donate them to a shelter.

5. Pay college-application fees for high-school students.

6. Donate your old car to a single mother without a car (or to a senior citizen or college student).

7. Sell any items you may not need on eBay or
Craigslist; create a scholarship-fund account for a
good cause in a foreign country.

8. Give stock shares to top-performing low-income college graduates in your community.

9. Pay a deserving high-school student's phone bill for a year while he or she is working toward college.

10. Donate old computers, iPads, or other devices to nonprofits and shelters.

I try to be the person I needed when I was down.
People need a consistent person they can count on. If
nothing else a person that can aspire to be like.

—Reginald Cotton, founder of Charity Contributors
of Chicago

God gives me an opportunity every morning to do
good and give back to those in need. That is enough
motivation to get me through even the toughest days.

—Sandi Torres, cofounder of Charity Contributors of
Chicago

11. Load a department-store gift card with cashed coins to give to a single mom for back-to-school supplies.

12. Purchase gift cards for cancer patients to enjoy something they love once a month (with a personal note).

13. Pay a medical bill for a cancer patient.

14. Underwrite equipment or part of equipment cost
for aspiring film directors or photographers.

15. Donate funds to purchase beds at your local
shelter.

16. Donate old televisions to local schools and
nonprofits.

17. Book a flight for inner-city youth and their family to visit somewhere they've never been.

18. Open an interest-bearing account in the name of your community, organization, or business to help the families of those killed due to domestic violence or police brutality; use the funds to assist with the burial.

19. Have a bake sale with children in your community and use the proceeds to go to a cause of their choice.

Every little bit helps. I'm motivated to give back—despite the overwhelming need—by the sheer acknowledgement of seeing some progress versus none at all. Giving back, regardless of the breath is still worthwhile because of the depth in impact you can make. It gives you the ability to change what you can, be an example to others, and encourage them to do the same—no matter the amount or reach. We can't conquer the mountain without step one.

—Victoria Watkins, Esq., founder of The Baffled Blog

20. Use your employer's match program to support a local cause.

21. Volunteer with friends, family, or your spouse at a local soup kitchen (year-round).

22. Recycle cans and use the funds to purchase healthy snacks for an after-school program.

23. Minimize one weekly payment for a month to use for supporting a good GoFundMe cause.

24. Purchase Girl Scout cookies for children in
cancer-treatment/therapy hospitals.

25. Pay registration fees for high-school students; contact the school counselor and accounting department.

26. Purchase toys throughout the year to give to parents for children's birthdays; contact your local shelter or school social workers.

27. Purchase gift cards to local prescription stores to give to seniors and the ill throughout the year.

28. Purchase or pay for bus cards, groceries, Internet service, or phone service for the recently laid off (up to six months or whatever you can do).

29. Purchase gym memberships for recent college graduates once they are hired, requiring they do the same for someone else.

100 Ways to Make a Difference Right Where You Are with What You Have

Altruism is self actualization of your mind, body, and soul.

—Colby Chapman MSEd, founder of PennyUp

30. Donate to a local soup kitchen.

31. Pay booth rent for a single-parent cosmologist or barber (first week, month, etc.).

32. Help pay tuition for a young person interested in starting barber school; request that he or she help another student once he or she is stable.

33. Purchase software or a conference ticket for an aspiring writer, doctor, or entrepreneur.

34. Collect blankets and comforters to leave with homeless people in the winter.

35. Write a list of people you know in need and a list of people with resources; consult each when an opportunity arises.

36. Commit to helping one high-school student find a
job or get into college at least once every three years;
follow up.

37. Purchase office supplies for an underfunded nonprofit.

38. Underwrite a counseling session for an uninsured single mom, homeless teen, or grieving parent.

39. Purchase a life-insurance policy for a low-income
senior, single mother, or unemployed millennial.

One of the most important reasons for giving back to me is LEGACY. Not from an egotistical sense in regards to what people will think of me, but more so in regards to what I leave behind for my son and those around me. A lot of people solely associate inheritance with the idea of wealth and currency, but I think about it in terms of value. In my eyes that is what truly defines a legacy, the value that is left behind for others to build on. With that, I intend to create a legacy established in giving and altruism my son can be proud of and use a guiding force for his own journey. That is what motivates me to give back.

—Todd Walton, managing director of FAME Enterprises

40. Purchase a one-year subscription to *Black Enterprise* for young aspiring entrepreneurs.

41. Purchase a membership to BLUE1647.com for a student or aspiring entrepreneur.

42. Underwrite the gas or light bill for a nonprofit once a year.

43. Volunteer for Feeding My Starving Children.

44. Purchase a laptop for a high-school senior going to college or pursuing a trade.

45. Purchase a one-hundred-dollar gift card and use it to provide acts of kindness throughout the month for the homeless, a mentee, purchasing gas for someone stranded, lunch for subway musicians, and so on.

46. Collect pennies throughout the month and donate
to PennyUp (PennyUp.org) at the end of the month.

47. Purchase a prom dress for the daughter of a single mother.

48. Pay for Inc. or LLC for an up-and-coming
nonprofit or entrepreneur.

49. Provide a special dinner or movie to a local group home once a month.

We have to live and operate with the spirit of abundance. There's always something to offer even if it's not money. We were blessed to blessed and it will come around. Have faith.

—Troy Pryor, founder of Creative Cypher Inc.

50. Purchase a gas card for a nonprofit after-school
program or senior center's vans or buses.

51. Pay one tuition bill (last month) for a top-performing student in private school with a single or ill parent.

52. Donate a vacation to a single parent (working two jobs or working and going to school) or to a nonprofit executive director or operating staff.

53. Donate an iPad or laptop to a nonprofit director or CEO.

Collecting, cleaning, and donating shoes to a local shelter for
Kicks4TheCity.

54. Keep an extra pair of adult (men's and women's)
shoes in your car at all times (socks too).

*Check out Kicks4TheCity and their nationwide
initiative to give back shoes to the homeless.

55. Keep toiletry bags to give away to the homeless in your car.

56. Wash the laundry of homeless people once a
week, month, and so on. This would be a great
opportunity for large groups.

57. Purchase storage units for nonprofits.

58. Purchase used hotel furniture for small businesses or nonprofits.

59. Donate travel mileage to nonprofit directors for charity-related travel.

The more I gave, the more I received! It's not in just giving alone, but it's the spirit in the giving is where you see the breakthroughs.

—Quinton Love, owner of Turkey Chop Chicago

60. Donate postage to nonprofit organizations.

*In some instances, it may be better to donate items over funds to organizations, as nonprofits have budgets for certain line items. They still have to use a certain amount of their budget for specific things, but having more of an item will keep them from having to cut back in that area (e.g., postage, supplies, travel, etc.).

Note: Administrative cost is where there is the greatest need; this expense may not be covered in a grant, or a very minimal percentage is covered.

61. Underwrite the cost of newsletter subscriptions for small businesses or nonprofits.

62. Sponsor a field trip for youth to attend a historical or educational event during the summer or school year.

63. Become an angel investor to organizations that
have received little or no grant funding and are within
their first one to three years of service.

64. Purchase auto-repair vouchers to local repair shops for single mothers.

65. Purchase AAA memberships for single mothers
and seniors.

66. Recycle from your workplace and donate the funds at the end of the year.

67. Donate time or effort to Black Celebrity Giving.

68. Sponsor the health-care bill of migrant farm workers (check rural clinic and hospital listings).

69. Identify one country to visit every year and donate at least one day of your visit to help where it's needed most. (Please do research beforehand to ensure your safety.)

I am so grateful for the various ways that clients, family and friends have supported me, my business and our book series. The support received carries us through the ups and downs of owning a business. Additionally, it fills my heart to know that others care, which in turn motivates me to give back, volunteer and support others' businesses and endeavors. It's a wonderful cycle of receiving with grace, and being full of gratitude.

—Julie Holloway, creator of JMH Art & Design Studio

70. Sponsor a low-income college student's trip abroad.

71. Help renovate and maintain upkeep of shelters for men, women, and families.

72. Collect food from five-star restaurants at the end of the night to deliver to homeless people.

73. Purchase bulk tickets to new black movie releases and give them to shelters, senior centers, or after-school programs.

74. Create a blog or vlog or use your social-media platforms to promote causes that you support.

75. Donate to local high-school band, traveling, or uniform expenses.

76. Donate one hour a week or month to help children learn how to read, spell, start a business, or succeed in STEM.

77. Create a "seed money" account to support teenpreneurs between the ages of ten and sixteen.

It was humbling to be a part of Camrin's story and play a part in having his wish granted by the Make-A-Wish Foundation (Chicago). Camrin has a unique developmental delay that affects his motor skills.

78. Volunteer with the Make-A-Wish Foundation.

79. Create a decorative jar or box to place in your home. Drop money (any amount) in this jar whenever you do something that you have vowed not to do or for things that you are disciplining yourself not to do. At the end of each month, collect those funds and put them in an account for the end of the year or use what you have to donate to a good cause. Ideally, you won't have a lot of cash in there, but if you do, it can turn a negative activity into something positive for you and your family.

I couldn't build a school, so I donated 6,000 books.

—Jeff Bridges, owner of Bridges Transportation, Moving and Cleaning.

80. Donate books to a local barber shop for children.

Check out Books with Barbers.

81. Donate videography or photography services to
an organization that is helping your community; help
them spread their message visually.

82. Provide free classes at a local community center or online for something that you are good at.

83. Buy and give out bus cards at local bus stops. There are people who spend nearly a third of their paycheck to purchase bus and train fare for their commute. These commutes are sometimes several hours and require multiple rides (more fare). This act of kindness may only lift the burden one day, but it will definitely help.

84. Volunteer at your local campaign office.

85. Purchase a one-year membership for a child to attend an after-school program (or summer).

86. Donate books to Books for Africa.

87. Adopt an inner-city street to keep up or invest
resources in.

88. Help seniors and those with disabilities get or maintain upgrades for home and apartment ramps.

89. Join your local chamber of commerce.

Donda's House Inc., would not be as successful as we are without the support of others. Support comes in many ways, through people making key introductions for us, through in-kind donations like offering our artists performance & employment opportunities, and even something as simple as "liking" or sharing social-media posts. Support is essential, because it is an acknowledgement of the problem(s) that we are trying to tackle, and a reinforcement of a solution and pathway forward.

One of my mentors, Mrs. Marian Wright Edelman says, "Service is the rent we pay for being. It is the very purpose of life, and not something that you do in your spare time." Many low-income and communities of color have experienced gentrification and divestment, which has resulted in class division. Success is often predicated on one's ability to "escape" or "make it out," of said communities resulting in concentrated poverty. Giving back can come in many forms—it can come through giving of one's time, one's money and one's resources. Once you find something that you are passionate about— arts & culture, mentoring, education, etc., find an organization that you can support and do what you can. If enough people do that, we will see more positive in our communities.

I am the woman that I am today because of people who decided to give back. I grew up in Kansas City,

Missouri, with a mother who was incarcerated and addicted to drugs. I had teachers, who took time outside of the classroom to expose me to new things. In the sixth Grade, I participated in a Children's Defense Fund Program called Freedom Schools, and I would not have been able to attend college if it weren't for a federally funded program called Upward Bound. I am motivated to give back, because I know that I don't personally or individually have the capacity to address the overwhelming need, but I do have the power and the ability to do something. When my something, combines with the somethings of other people, it creates an overwhelming response to the need, and that motivates me. I am very interested in cultivating leadership and philanthropists that serve the communities that they come from. While advocates are important, I am interested in helping youth & their families develop agency over their own lives—to speak and advocate for themselves and their needs.

—Donnie Smith, executive director of Donda's House

90. Support Charity Contributors of Chicago
(www.CharityContributors.com).

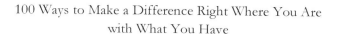

91. Pay off day-care bill balances at your local twenty-four-hour day-care center for children who have to stay overnight. There are many mothers who are struggling to work late-night shifts, often spending most of their funds to pay for day care.

92. Provide a spa basket with a gift card to moms who utilize twenty-four-hour day-care centers.

93. Purchase a basketball rim for local inner-city kids in the summer. High-crime areas are often the result of children and young adults not having anything to do.

94. Set aside $500 every year to give to a local family-owned business.

95. Donate care packages to young mothers who are giving their babies away for adoption.

96. Join or support 100 Black Men initiatives. Check
for local chapters at 100BlackMen.org.

97. Support HBCU Wall Street initiatives
(www.hbcuwallstreet.com).

98. Support my philanthropy apparel line, Brand Ministry Apparel. Proceeds from all sells go to various charities, many of which are included in this book. To learn more or to submit your organization to be considered for donations from Brand Ministry Apparel, visit VauveAnais.com.

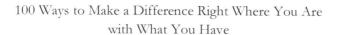

99. Donate to the Class of 2003 Scholarship. This is a
cause near and dear to my heart. I am the product of
a single-parent home as well as Proviso East High
School. As a result, I am drawn to helping single
parents and their children who go to Proviso East.

If you organize your life around your passion, you can turn your passion into your story; then turn your story into something bigger. Something that matters.

—Sam DeSalu, social entrepreneur and owner of De Salu Naturals

100. Pray for those who dedicate their lives to giving back.

Pray for social-change leaders.

Pray for nonprofit founders.

Pray for community activists.

Pray for philanthropists and humanitarians.

It's not always easy to dedicate your life to service. Being a vessel that God uses to help people may present many challenges during the journey. Those who dedicate their lives to giving back often have the most dysfunctional homes and families. Those who dedicate their lives to giving back are often emotionally and mentally burdened; the empathy we possess can't be turned on and off. This book has actually inspired me to write a book about the life of a humanitarian. I won't give away too much, but I hope these tips will empower you to give right where you are with what you have, and if you already give above and beyond, I hope it inspires you to get creative and think outside the box.

ABOUT THE AUTHOR

 Vau've Anais Davis, founder of Official Anais PR, a Chicago-based public-relations consulting firm, is an award-winning philanthropist and first-generation entrepreneur who aspires to build a brand legacy through business development and community service.

After graduating from the University of Illinois at Urbana-Champaign with her bachelor of science degree in psychology, Davis had a chance to put her passion and natural talent for helping others into action at two nonprofit youth organizations.

In her many roles, she helped develop, execute, and promote social services, after-school programs for teens, and career-development services. She also assisted with the production of an HIV-awareness campaign film. She has helped secure over $1,000,000 in grants, planned and marketed events, and solicited sponsorships from individuals and corporations.

Her innate ability to connect people and concepts to achieve desired goals prompted Davis to launch Official Anais Consulting (formerly Official Anais PR) in 2010. The purpose of her firm is twofold: to elevate the brands of local entrepreneurs, small businesses, and nonprofits to national and international levels; and to give back to the community.

Davis's "Charity Corner" blog and her annual toy drive are two of her most prized charitable projects. She understands that it is challenging for nonprofit entities to market their programs and good deeds effectively with small budgets and even smaller staffs; therefore, she features two organizations or charities bimonthly on her blog with the goal of giving them exposure and soliciting donations for causes that serve communities throughout Illinois and the Greater Chicagoland areas.

Additionally, for the past several years, Official Anais Consulting has hosted annual toy drives to support single mothers during Christmas, one of the hardest times of the year for some parents. Due to overwhelming need, the firm hosted two toy drives during the third and fourth years. Support for Davis's charitable efforts was so great that she was also able to donate to a mentoring organization as well as a domestic-violence shelter in Englewood.

In September 2013, Davis launched the Shark Tank Social, "one of Chicago's hottest events," according to the *Examiner*. Highly regarded by Chicago influencers, community leaders, and entrepreneurs, this monthly networking event connects budding entrepreneurs and other professionals who have a business idea that they want to pitch to investors. Some even consider auditioning for the actual show.

Davis has received several awards and recognitions for her professional and charitable contributions to local entrepreneurs, small businesses, and nonprofit organizations. In 2013, Official Anais PR was awarded the "Best Non-Profit PR and Event Planning Firm" by Black Celebrity Giving. The firm also received a "Humanitarian Award" from Fashion Arts & Humanitarian Fetes. Davis has been recognized as one of the "Most Powerful Women on the South Side of Chicago" for her contributions to the community.

In 2016, Davis launched a philanthropy apparel line called Brand Ministry Apparel and started a scholarship fund for her high-school alma mater, Proviso East High School, located in Maywood, Illinois.

In addition to her own ventures, Davis contributes to Stellar Award winner Mark Hubbard's Gospel radio show with her "Purpose, PR, and Philanthropy" segment. She serves as community-relations director of Speak Hope Inc. and serves on the leadership team of Creative Cypher Inc.

Made in the USA
Columbia, SC
04 October 2018